Celebration on Joyful, Joyful, We Adore Thee

Sw. Full
Gt. Full, Sw. to Gt., Ch. to Gt.
Ch. Full
Ped. Full, Sw. to Ped., Ch. to Ped.

Rhonda Furr
based on HYMN TO JOY
by Ludwig van Beethoven

Allegro spiritoso (♩ = 108)
7
Solo
10
13
marcato
16

rit.
Legato (♩ = 88)
Sw. Flute 8', 4', 2'
(no Ped.)
rit.
(♩ = 117)
Gt. Principal 8', 4', Sw. to Gt.
Sw.

38
42
rit.
46
accelerando
Gt.
Add
Maestoso (♩ = 101)
Add
51

55
accelerando
59
Tempo I (♩ = 83)
rit.
Full
63
66
molto rit.

Allegro (♩ = 105)
68
Add
70
Ped. +Reeds
72
74

76
6
78
(♯)
82
84
2
4
4
4

86
88
8va
91
(8va)
93
(8va)
sfz
poco accel.
rit.